I Mean

I MEAN
Kate Colby

Ugly Duckling Presse
Brooklyn, 2015

First Edition, First Printing, 2015
Edition of 1200

Ugly Duckling Presse
The Old American Can Factory
232 Third Street #E-303
Brooklyn, NY 11215

Cover art: *Montana Night* by Victoria Burge
Design by Don't Look Now! and Doormouse

This book is made possible in part by a grant from the
National Endowment for the Arts.

Ugly Duckling Presse is a member of the Community
of Literary Magazines and Presses and a 501(c)(3)
registered nonprofit. Tax-deductible donations are
welcome.

www.uglyducklingpresse.org

National
Endowment
for the Arts
arts.gov

ART WORKS.

CONTENTS

I Mean

I mean to say

I mean I keep meaning to

I mean amending

I mean correcting

I mean qualifying

I mean collecting

I mean $X + X + X$
and so forth

I mean all possible values

I mean adding

I mean and also

I mean pileups happen
when you can't see
where you're going

I mean where you are

I mean your hand
in front of your face

I mean my hand

I mean if that's all
I can see

I mean if that's all
I'm looking at

I mean that's not all

I mean there is no end

I mean this isn't the beginning

I mean only means

I mean blow the house down
with breathlessness

I mean a house of breathlessness

I mean the walls
are braced
against themselves

I mean brace yourself

I mean to take the house down
with its own components

I mean throw the whole deck at it

I mean two-by-fours and oven mitts

I mean rocks
hucking them
at walls of rocks

I mean self-healing walls

I mean with insipid pocks

I mean BB dings in street signs

I mean bullet holes in stop signs

I mean to riddle

I mean all signs point to "yes"

I mean eyelids are designed to admit some light

I mean sound

I mean boom

I mean faster than gravity

I mean I am not equal to the work

I mean I'm over my head

I mean hovering

I mean levitating

I mean light as a feather
wide as a plane

I mean fight as a feather
(infinitesimally)

I mean I'm going to talk about it

I mean talk about it
by talking about
talking about it

I mean write about it

I mean scrape it all towards me
with the edge of my hand

I mean like a spray of crumbs

I mean pile

I mean to pile up
and get on top of

I mean for the prospect

I mean for the pea
beneath the mattress

I mean to feel the ceiling

I mean to figure it
like a mime

I mean just imagine it

I mean kiss it

I mean I'm already running out of air

I mean steam

I mean fire

I mean fight it

I mean feed

I mean with fire

I mean fire
is not finite
only fuel

I mean light
is not finite
only illumination

I mean things to illuminate

I mean to throw shadows

I mean I have an important
question: is this important?

I mean there are no stupid questions
only precarious piles of them

I mean I don't think

I mean I have my work
cut out

I mean découpage

I mean to decorate empty boxes

I mean mountains of them

I mean to make mountains of them

I mean I like to see
the whole horizon

I mean just putting it out there

I mean the horizon
is where I see it

I mean where does a mountain end
and everything else begin?

I mean the foothills

I mean the valley

I mean the sky

I mean how far from my head

I mean I know there are names
but I don't want to know them

I mean everything is of a piece

I mean right now

I mean a meteorite slashes through
atmosphere, roof, ceiling, lands
on the living room rug and smolders

I mean in front of the television

I mean there's a smoking hole in the rug
and a laugh track

I mean *Mork & Mindy*

I mean *mise en abyme*

I mean playing people playing people

I mean sets within sets of themselves

I mean I dream about myself

I mean I've canceled myself out

I mean I'm over here
while you're staring at
the smoldering hole in the rug
where you thought I was

I mean a black grid on a white field
and the fuzzy gray dots where the lines cross
that you can see but not look at

I mean "slippage"

I mean the slip-proof dots
on the baby's socks

I mean things for which
names may or may not exist

I mean there are names
for what you are and for who

I mean names for things
that don't or no longer exist

I mean kicking bones
down the stairs
they're in my way

I mean in the desert

I mean everything is contained

I mean bound

I mean imminent

I mean right now

I mean immanence

I mean all at once

I mean an infinitely subdividing distance
from your face

your hand

I mean your frame

I mean immanence of adolescence,
winter sunset behind bare branches.
In a car. Cat Stevens.

I mean you can't make this shit up

I mean it's Cartesian

I mean the sum

I mean gestalt

I mean more

I mean soul

I mean stab
pen through paper

I mean repeatedly

I mean stomata
let the light through

I mean oven mitts
are words

I mean syntactic units

I mean tools

I mean means

I mean oven-mitt puppet theater

I mean in the round

I mean all the walls
are see-through

I mean no one can see the light
is coming from the wrong direction

I mean the aisle lighting
is on the ceiling

I mean the walls
don't meet the ceiling

I mean the sky

I mean the ends of the earth

I mean there are ways to get around them

I mean get over them

I mean with a kind of stile

I mean pile
of individually useless tools

I mean poems as piles
of perfume test strips

I mean litmus strips
in innumerable labs
of trash cans

I mean the letter-shaped
spaces in my correction tape

I mean dead letters
denoting notes

I mean chords

I mean to correct the bad ones

I mean the bad one

I mean the only chord I know
is differently bad each time

I mean except when I hit it

I mean I go limp in my own arms

I mean it's major

I mean in motion

I mean pictures

I mean the moment
a woman exhales
and slides beneath
her mounds of bubbles

I mean mountains

I mean hill beyond hill beyond hill

I mean the boundaries of the kingdom
I can see

I mean the periphery
is a circle and I am
seldom at its center

I mean except when I am

I mean the circumference
of sound

I mean a plane
crossing the sky

I mean how long does it take?

I mean how far away is the furthest
visible point in a cloudless sky

I mean the furthest visible cloud
in the cloud cover

I mean as far as the eye can see

I mean define

I mean the horizon is the shape of the eye

I mean is the lake the shape of its shoreline
or the shoreline the shape of the lake?

I mean the same
of me and my skin

I mean bodies of water
become their shores

I mean everything is round
and around you

I mean everything takes shape
of itself

I mean shapes come to look like
the shapes they once stood for

I mean five-pointed stars
and six

I mean what we divine there

I mean everything is pointing

I mean in Jodhpur there are three
different reasons given for
the walls being blue. Depends
who you ask. Nobody remembers.

I mean some things are blue as Jodhpur

I mean 1:1:1

I mean more than authenticity

I mean true blue

I mean verdigris

I mean which is the natural state of a surface,
the patina or the polish?

I mean ore or artifact

I mean mud flaps with sexy silhouettes

I mean having it made

I mean for you? Half price.

I mean you really had to be there
and were
is the new picaresque

I mean access with lingering
whiff of difficulty

I mean fare thee
forward

I mean no sleep is never enough

I mean I'm not sure I want to think this hard

I mean if I could only lie

I mean still

I mean waking up to snow
you weren't expecting to fall

I mean white out

I mean it's falling
into shapes

I mean the way you see it

I mean snow falling
into men and angels

I mean chalk outlines

I mean white branches

I mean bent branches

I mean thin limbs are
too small to not withstand
the weight

I mean to break

I mean land
mimicking the land-
scaping

I mean topiary mountains

I mean thirteen ways
of being a blackbird

I mean the unblinking eye
of all the snowy mountains

I mean a range

I mean in circles

I mean in the likeness
of my looking glass

I mean camera lucida

I mean portraiture

I mean the longest distance
between two points

I mean the difficult drape and fold of fabric

I mean the difficulty of folding
a fitted sheet

I mean the figure written
out by the grass near the lens

I mean a smudge on the lens
upstaging the world

I mean the most local world
still has problems of scale

I mean weight

I mean to reduce it
in the mathematical sense

I mean to condense

I mean my name
on a grain of rice

I mean to make it
easily digestible

I mean to reduce it
in the culinary sense

I mean boil it down

I mean until falling from the bone

I mean to render

I mean eat your heart out

I mean every success
is a simulated drowning

I mean saturation
is not sustainable

I mean to do
the dead-man's
or survival
float and be
swept to sea

I mean I'm a vessel
ripped from its mooring
when the tide pulls away

I mean the line
burns through my hands

I mean then it snaps

I mean then I'm dashed

I mean wrecked

I mean personal disaster

I mean a flood
leaves fetid pools of itself
in contiguous, separate cellars

I mean cells

I mean with bars

I mean nets

I mean reticula

I mean cells
within cells
and so on

I mean so forth

I mean sets within sets
receding

I mean nesting

I mean reproducing

I mean scale models
of scale models

I mean pocket-sized
arks of everything
in triplicate

I mean half of it matches

I mean the rest of it goes
because it's already there

I mean like leap seconds

I mean contaminants

I mean the moon is off

I mean it no longer goes

I mean sunlight is only made
visible by moisture

motes

I mean mites
and that it barely passes for a homonym

I mean there's an actual
kind of bush called "burning"

I mean I'm just saying

I mean you can pile words up
and wrap the referents around them

I mean that's all you can do

I mean I do try to
"wrap my mind around" things
I'm okay with that phrase

I mean I once saw Martha Stewart
wrap a turkey in puff pastry on TV

I mean it looked great

I mean the meat
(it hardly holds the blood anymore)

I mean last meals
I plan mine when I'm hungry
Bolognese and a good glass of red

I mean white

I mean ham

I mean a wan bit of pear in red Jell-O

I mean to hang

I mean to be
of two minds

I mean more

I mean dividing

I mean now I'm a can of fruit cocktail

I mean pastry—a mille-mille-
infinity millefeuille
picked apart into its only
individually translucent layers

I mean planes

I mean if planes could coexist with light

I mean "interstitial"
is a word I use knowingly

I mean flinchingly

I mean "curvature," "slippage," Möbius strips

I mean geometry is wanting

I mean wishful

I mean words are

I mean wedged into the world
and made to work

I mean poetry

I mean pi in the sky

I mean a horizon
is only how you see it

I mean I see to see
in circles

I mean they're insidious

viscous

I mean the teeth are
on the outside

I mean I want my circumference
and to eat it too

I mean to be bigger than you

I mean contain more

I mean mean more

I mean with infinite density

I mean singularity

I mean aleph-infinity

I mean on the largest scale

I mean ontogeny, phylogeny, the camera
panning out from microbe to cosmos

I mean cochlear recapitulation of seashells

I mean fractals and vice-versa.
Seaweed. Galaxies.

I mean it's a long shot

I mean what I thought was the ocean
is only my body

I mean either a vase or two faces

I mean most illusion is optical
preference

I mean for figure or field

I mean a mirage
is dependent upon
both sea and sky
but not neither

I mean to morph
from sky to sea
and the life forms found
in their negative spaces

I mean on both hands (and each
is drawing the other)

I mean hand over fist

I mean hand over hand

I mean hoisting

I mean pulling up anchor

letting go
of the mooring, being
sucked from the cove

I mean to drift

I mean drown

I mean cancel myself out

I mean my life raft
made to match
the roses on my bathing cap

I mean look out

look here

I mean I'm looking away

I mean until everything is
excluded

I mean it's exclusive

I mean I
am not one
of you
except as a member
of the set of all sets

I mean what if every moment
were allowed to unfold
like notes in a heady perfume

I mean wine

I mean with a hint of cinder,
ripe plum, clove and roses,
suggestion of leather
(I don't mean sex)

I mean to unfold forever

I mean in suspension

I mean just think of all
the neglected information
crushing in from the edges

I mean gasping against the glass
in a subway or stadium stampede

I mean when you can't breathe

I mean what is that thing about learning
to live in the moment by taking an hour
to eat a Cheerio?

I mean what if there's a dark bird outside
and it's moving

I mean two ways about it

I mean more than anything
there's no time

I mean just to stay afloat

I mean by moving and making
wavelets

I mean concentric circles
overlapping
what else I might mean

I mean circles come in different sizes—
the locust tree grows and drops its black
creaky bean pods only every two years

I mean I keep finding the leaves
in the baby's mouth

I mean plagues of locusts
and their inscrutable cycles
(I don't mean God)

I mean red tides
of microbic blooms

I mean reading the circulars
and buying what you find there

I mean comestible life cycles

I mean Peek Freans and Andes Candies

I mean things can resurface

I mean ironically

I mean with a twist

I mean the conveyor belt slips
and becomes a Möbius strip

I mean a Möbius globe
where every revolution leaves you
inside where you started

I mean on the other side
of the glass

I mean two-way mirror

I mean the interrogation
lamp on the landscape

in backlight

I mean the light
from behind the eyes

I mean all the eyes

I mean everything is the same
but from different angles

I mean everything is different
from the same angle

I mean from where I'm standing

I mean every beach
is the end of the whole ocean

I mean I contain it

I mean with my own dimensions

I mean to induce them

I mean by induction

I mean reduction
to myself

I mean I have my work
to cut out

I mean what is the depth of a surface?

I mean the volume

I mean to drill to the core
and drop a microphone down

I mean hammer

I mean I hear hollow sounds—
waves breaking on dead reef,
the edges of the island, blue,
calving ice masses

I mean cubes against glass

I mean the sound of how I hear
in my head. From the outside
stringy weeds insinuate, dampen,
expand into and grow over me.

I mean the backseat feeling of Jim Croce

I mean the kind of backseat
where your parents are in the front

I mean genius loci
you'll never understand
I *love* this song

I mean the *Peanuts* theme

I mean do your ears hang low

I mean home
is a quality of light

I mean the jang of sleigh bells on a front door
pulled closed with haste and effort. Warm lamps,
smell of roast, tinkle of ice against glass, laughter
from the kitchen. Stamping your feet, breathing
and brushing the snow off.

I mean I want to write Christmas

I mean just keep
stacking mattresses

I mean shoving my hand between them
all the way up to the shoulder

I mean to find a key
to the city
that actually affords access

I mean to what it's made of—
keening correspondents
with real news

I mean joy and flattened
Drumstick wrappers

I mean landscape is bound
because we are in it

I mean at night I feel mountains
when I'm in the mountains

I mean what I thought was the ocean
is only the breaking berm of my body

I mean the city has a hinge
it's just stuck in the closed position

I mean stuck like care instructions
into native vegetation.
Plastic stakes. Deep roots.

I mean for what I am rooting

I mean for all the fruitless pits
impaled in winter windows

I mean a continuous roll
of sod, unrolling

I mean a quilt
of every street sign in the city
every city
stitched together and unrolled in a field

I mean I'd like to see that

I mean to write that

I mean to write like an angel
with a fleshy tongue

I mean to write in blood
with a splintered tongue depressor

I mean this bloody work
is all I know how to do

I mean the stab
I know to take

I mean to dab at it

I mean my pulse points
stink of applied ink

I mean correction fluid

I mean my own blood
and my fingerprints in it

I mean the world is round
and around with itself

I mean it turns and gathers itself
like line on a winch

I mean like a winch

I mean cotton candy

I mean a gathering eddy
of international treaties
personal resolutions
old leaves

I mean infinite layers
of nacre
around infinite irritants

I mean coils
neat and increasing

I mean an endless length of thread
with a single knot knotting
over and over again

I mean on top of itself

I mean into itself

I mean my mouth
bristling with
expectant pins

I mean it's a pincushion

my head

I mean the hammer in my hand

I mean tools
heaped like bones
in a catacomb

I mean the master's house
hoarding itself

I mean with boundless carpets
of needles

I mean drawers
full of packages
of cocktail napkins

I mean taste-made habits

I mean induced reflex

I mean with a rubber hammer

I mean genius tempus

I mean I'm designing this
dress while I'm wearing it

I mean don't look back
(dog-doo on your shoe)

I mean severe tire damage

I mean just look at
the dirt you've tracked in

I mean all the time
capsules pull at my neck
like heavy matte-black pearls

I mean lost black
boxes of words

I mean at the bottom of the sea

I mean you don't know what you're missing

I mean that you're missing

I mean I'm missing

I mean me

I mean reflexively
je me manque
and on and on
eternally

I mean I'm back
in a convoluted feedback loop

I mean a small eddy
at the edge of an important river

I mean everything moves by
while I'm stuck here dividing
cell over cell

I mean till I burst
inside my own confines

I mean a grave
gets emptier with time

I mean that time
takes it all up

I mean it displaces

I mean it's petulantly
kicking at my shin

I mean my bones

I mean we haven't
received proper burial

I mean there's a mist
on the lens

I mean the image

I mean breath

I'm looking
into the wrong end

I mean again

I mean it's absurd

I mean like a play

I mean on a screen

I mean I recuse myself
from my interests

I mean they're conflicted

I mean all over the place

I mean static

I mean someone's messed
with my presets

I mean my homemade antenna

my forced appendage
of paper and bones

I mean it hurts by pointing

I mean fever and attendant
sensitivity to sound—
heat, pulse, bird,
shrill silence of the middle
distance

I mean referred pain
behind the ears

I mean the tenderness of skin
around sutures

I mean to stitch
the wound from the inside

I mean inside-out

I mean the bare unpainted
backs of places

I mean with joists
of metaphor, sealant
of mirrors

I mean a joint
is distorting

I mean it only looks right
at night
by refrigerator light

I mean it only works when you need it

I mean on a need-to-see basis

I mean all the never-seen
facets of Everest

I mean vision is a faculty

I mean facility

I mean institùtional
doors swing both ways

I mean in only two directions

I mean identity or diagnosis

I mean my deafness

I mean the feedback
from my hearing aid

I mean the ping
of the rigging

I mean flagpoles
in the wind

I mean the sound
that says advance
the frame

I mean the reel
of a bridge flickering

I mean breaking

under duress
of music

I mean supersonic harmonics

I mean frequency

I mean rate of occurrence

I mean rapidly

I mean it's trilling

I mean in the highest C

I mean how slight can a nuance be

I mean the lowest notes
are already barely distinguishable

I mean there's little perceivable difference

I mean the difference is merely technical

I mean a drawbridge can be stuck
in the up position

I mean a bridge only by definition
and the opposite—all non-existent
bridges (not dividing or bridging
difference)

I mean one wants everything
but wouldn't want to live there.

I mean one also wants nothing
and can't have it

I mean to disappear

I mean transcend

I mean transcendentalists

I mean rows of pews and bare
branches in high windows,
smell of heat, consommé.
Hymns.

I mean immanence

I mean inscape

I mean names
still exist like empty
collection plates

I mean for whom
they are collecting

I mean Icarus Iscariot

I mean historical portmanteau

I mean when things go together
that aren't together
the world snaps flat

I mean the telescope collapses
all eyes on deck

I mean the splattering sound
of air escaping through the end

I mean the end whose purpose is
to inflate

I mean the need to equilibrate

I mean in California the heart soars,
in New England it beats against
its chambers

I mean there are different kinds of elation

I mean biting a yellow wooden pencil
the bitter gray taste of it

I mean how many more times in your life
will you bite a pencil or swim in the ocean?

I mean what if you knew the answer

I mean actual shadows in old sun

I mean new light
is usually artificial

I mean Edison bulbs
with big glowing filaments
and retromancy writ lit

I mean antique houses
with vinyl siding
keeping the elements discrete

I mean class action
taken by every class

I mean class action
taken by members of multiple classes

I mean all impossible
combinatoric classes
(dividing till no difference is
a dead end)

I mean an instrument of ice
the sound of the medium
melting

I mean even though I can't
play it that way

I mean every new word the baby learns
heals a pinhole

I mean seals

I mean Bacos, "the crispy garnish
that tastes just like its name"

I mean by the time I get there
someone's always already
pulled the ball away

I mean the measured
stipple of my stave

eyes to the grindstone

I mean I don't want to know
any more constellations.
The night sky is flat.

I mean collapsed

I mean star maps dissolve
into workaday sunspots

I mean never take pictures
that's all you'll remember

I mean you can't pay
attention to everything

I mean in isolation

I mean all at once

I mean you have to
favor meter or meaning

I mean time or space

I mean though I'd like to
include everything and
simultaneously

I mean to suggest everything—
you can only walk to Chateaubriand's grave
when the tide is low. Salt-stunted
grass grows about him and his head,
at his suggestion, is turned toward
the sea (I don't mean "ocean")

I mean romance

I mean a brackish breeze,
reeking seaport, bilge, nets
brown and tangled with tannin

I mean a place of my own making

I mean a home away from home

I mean homing

I'm homing away

I mean between

I mean channeling

I mean red right returning

I mean from the open sea

I mean I am not equal to the work

I mean the work
in the form of its physical confines—
page, book, screen. Score.

I mean there
you have it

I mean a measure of a man

I mean this poem
to go on forever

I mean an endless unrolling
player-piano scroll

I mean I'd rather be the paper than the player

I mean the holes
denoting notes

I mean the music

I mean how it moves

I mean skin is so inconvenient

I mean how it heals

I mean how it sticks
with itself

I mean to leave it
in a heap on the floor
in a hot tryst with looking

I mean to overlook—
the sense of seeing into

I mean to overlook—
the sense of not seeing at all
and the opposite (at times I have
to hide behind my hands)

I mean as far as I can see—
the sense of what seems
to me to be

I mean as far as I can see
meaning horizon

I mean all the way

I mean further / more

I mean all the ways
I can think of and those I cannot

I mean I mean in all the ways I can think of

I mean I wish I could think of more

I mean mean more

I mean what if I deleted all the "I mean"s?

I mean I'm trying to overwrite

I mean both on top of and too much

I mean add that to the stack

I mean there's no end
of means

I mean theoretical means

I mean I still have to mean the baby
and he means me back

I mean put on your rain boots

I mean right now

I mean in real time

I mean man hours

I mean to instill some
absolute values

I mean some water
is more important
than other water

I mean $X \neq X$

I mean everything is unique

I mean every instance
of every thing is unique

I mean the whole universe
is unique

I mean singular

I mean singularity

I mean all the same

I mean the set of all sets
that is a member of itself

I mean I am my own alibi

I mean imposter

I mean fun fur

I mean a sparse and tonic-y combover

I mean I am not equal to the work

I mean incessant ingathering
isn't sustainable

I mean I'm bound to run out
of reachable crumbs

I mean then there's a leak

I mean light

bang

I mean till I burst

I mean how sewer gasses burp
into my bathroom

I mean my mother's bathroom

I mean my grandmother's bathroom

I mean my grandmothers' bathrooms

I mean with outspreading
lushness of a leach field

I mean I highly value delicacy
but have a habit of putting my feet up

I mean all landscapes are bathed
in some kind of light

I mean a thick cloud of gnats
is together too big, individually
too small for a net. Shut your mouth.
One wriggles and dies under the eyelid.

I mean it's something to see

I mean no-see-ums

I mean I can't see
what's in my eye

I mean in my sight

I mean the eye adapts

I mean eyes don't remember

I mean motion is required

I mean to perceive

I mean movement is the medium

I mean the mind does sort of dance

I mean to dance but still
keep trying to say it

I mean dance it off

I mean write it off

I mean out

I mean but it's different every time

I mean the way something can be
said or not said

I mean stabbed at

I mean to stab around it

I mean until it breaks
at the perforations

I mean landscape is made

I mean a surface sometimes seems

I mean seams

I mean sutures

grafts

I mean generation

I mean ripped-
off arms of starfish
growing more starfish

I mean teeming asunder

I mean the way water sounds

I mean in fountains

I mean the coins

I mean every word of them

I mean all the wishes

I mean to embody
their conglomerate qualities

I mean unspeakable horror
and unspeakable beauty

I mean them differently

I mean beauty can be made
of words but horror can only be named

I mean horror can't be abstracted

I mean it isn't abstract
and can't be made that way

I mean well-named horror can
be beautiful

I mean Wilfred Owen's poems
are neither horrific nor beautiful

I mean can beauty be named
or made but not both?

I mean a name turns to stone

I mean I'm totally making this up

I mean I don't know how to be a poet

I mean I'm a rebar Medusa

I mean cursed with endless construction

I mean with the dangers of addition

I mean maybe beauty can only be made
in the mirror

I mean mugging, kissy-faced,
pluckily marching in place
in the corner

I mean facing into the corner

I mean I've talked myself into

I mean thought myself

I mean the corner looks back

I mean reflects

I mean the corner is the chorus

I mean in the kind of song
where the verses are catchier than the chorus

I mean like "Feel Like Makin' Love"

I mean a song doesn't need a chorus

I mean refrain

I mean to endlessly modulate
with endless key changes

I mean every key
to every door I've ever had

I mean every phone number

I mean every phone number I've been
handed on a cocktail napkin

I mean all piled up

I mean they have all meant me at once

I mean at one time

I mean over time

I mean I wish I could remember them all

I mean look at them

I mean like a core
drilled from an iceberg

I mean trepanning
a core of memory

I mean to roll the eyes back
into the head and see

I mean what if I changed
"I mean" to "I need"

I mean "I want"

I mean "I believe"

I mean if I wrote these poems

I mean in addition

I mean would they collect
in similar fashions?

I mean radiate

I mean like a radiator
sibilant with pressure

I mean steam

I mean the small leak
that prevents an explosion

I mean how a let-go balloon
splutters around the room
with its own deflation

I mean to deflate toward

I mean to deflate forever

I mean let's just pretend
this poem never ends

I mean it continues

I mean it's continuous

I mean to come around again

I mean with a twist

I mean hitch

I mean setback

I mean with pools
of myself for self-
reflection

I mean back in the corner

I mean there's a frequent
need for reorientation

I mean because the medium
is moving

I mean the equipment

I mean sweat-stained tape
on the grip of my racquet

I mean its sticky medium
is stuck to
my hand

I mean hurling the racquet

I mean I'm hurling it at

I mean the weight of the racquet and
my resistant wrist-slash-pointing at

I mean the body means the object

I mean of the pointing

I mean the work

I mean the longest distance
between two points

I mean the shortest distance—
bring the ends together and wring
until frayed

I mean to wring the medium

I mean mangle

I mean my modus operandi

I mean mode of transportation

I mean with webs from the fingertips

I mean they shoot forth

I mean eyes bug
from jutting head

I mean being the body
doing the work

I mean being the work

I mean it's something to see

I mean writing in the tub ring
of cells and secretion

I mean to write the tub ring

I mean my feet pointing
through bubble-bath mountains

I mean as in dance

I mean thinness: see-
through to the bones

I mean *port de bras* of words
moving again and again
into musculature

I mean the unspeakable
entangled with cells, hair,
nails, thrust from fingertips

I mean it *bourrées* off the ends

I mean at least I can try
to say it *how* I mean it

I mean the manner in which I mean it

I mean "if I could say it I wouldn't
have to dance it"

I mean the muscle means the hand
and the word and the self-
identical sound of its creation

I mean a closed circuit

I mean infinite performance

I mean in every direction

I mean concentrically

I mean the audience
in the round

I mean to reflect the audience
(mirrors stand face-to-face
obviating eyes)

I mean a circuit has been closed

if one goes, they all go

I mean they're all already
there

I mean I chase my own ambulance

I mean I represent myself

I mean this pile is growing

I mean I'm whittling away
negative space with the shavings
(if only I could see what I'm carving)

I mean out of itself

I mean from the medium

I mean down to nothing

I mean to disappear

I mean Icarus
of infinite density

I mean drowning

I mean collapsing

I mean shut up
like a telescope

I mean to lick and
pinch the light out

I mean little black holes
in a field of light

I mean points
perforating starry night
gathers and folds into itself

I mean into the light

I mean you don't stop seeing
when your eyes are closed—
there's a black static
on the backs of the lids

I mean I've been dying
to tell you all of this

I mean everything
I'll take to the grave with me

I mean everything
I have no choice but to take

I mean everything
can't be left for posterity

I mean I've tried to take it all down

I mean thought about it

I mean like Samuel Pepys

I mean I'm not that interesting

I mean you clearly can't see me
behind these dark glasses
blinking

I mean landscape extends
only as far as the lens

I mean cranium

I mean the volume of the body

I mean the volume of this

I mean in a circle
and the content
of its circumference

I mean its negative

I mean it's inside out

I mean there's a twist

I mean in the ribbon

I mean the keys are
imprinting themselves

I mean the page is blank

I mean whited out

I mean overwritten

I mean with Correct-O-Type

I mean invisible palimpsest

I mean to flip it
and begin again

I mean square one
give or take a little

I mean $X = X$
plus or minus itself

I mean nothing
is the same as
nothing

I mean to make lemons of lemons

I mean lemons of lemons of lemons

I mean everything and more

I mean all at once

I mean all the time

I mean the sublime

I mean aleph-times-infinity

I mean the layer after landscape

I mean although I am in it

I mean it's contained within me

I mean umami

I mean ineffability

I mean editing can mean adding

I mean hammering

I mean plus one

I am not equal to the work

I mean I'm going to stay up all night
every night for the rest of my life

I mean no sleep is never enough

I mean this hammering
keeps me awake

I mean I'm pounding away
on the organ as it slowly
descends into the stage

I mean with my head
thrown back, eyes closed

I mean if this could extend
in all directions it would
still be but one flimsy layer
of an impossible optical pastry

I mean how would it end?
Phyllo houses on the moon.
No difference. The longest division.

The Longest Division

RAINBOW SWASH

Heading into the city from the south on Boston's Southeast Expressway, you pass a large white gas tank painted with a ragged rainbow. It looks like the work of a petulant giant.

The design looks very dated, which seems strange for something so minimal and innocuous. It was created in 1971 and reminds me of the carpeting in my pediatric dentist's office. Or a pair of contemporaneous sneakers. I can't quite say why it looks so thoroughly of its time, other than that the uncut colors on the bright white background have a pop-art quality. (I recently learned the difference between a tint and a shade—that the former characterizes a pure, baseline color with white added and the latter with black. I don't know how I lived so long without knowing this.)

Another factor that dates *Rainbow Swash*—or positions it in time, anyway—is the rumored presence of Ho Chi Minh's profile in the southerly edge of the blue stripe. I've known about this for years and have tried to see it every time I drive by, but finally looked up the image online in order to locate the face and telltale long beard. I see what everyone else sees, but can't say for sure that it's actually there.

Corita Kent, the progressive former nun who designed *Rainbow Swash*, always denied embedding the likeness of Ho Chi Minh. But in 1991 the old tank with the original mural was pulled down and *Rainbow Swash* was recreated on a new, adjacent tank, with Ho Chi Minh's supposed nose deliberately deemphasized. This change rendered the potential face less obvious in order to placate a protesting group of Vietnam veterans. Just to cover the bases, one of the painters hired to paint the new mural was an elderly Vietnamese survivor of the conflict.

Corita, as the artist was known, died of cancer in 1986. Her art is emblematic of the Vietnam War era and its optimistic design sensibilities, which bled into the 80s. The image with which she is most strongly associated is the swash-like "Love" stamp she created for the US Postal Service the year before she died. Looking at pictures of the stamp and the swash side by side, I notice that in both cases the rainbow's colors are somewhat out of order, although not in the same way, and that purple is always in its correct place, like a closing bracket. There's no indigo in optimism.

The most interesting thing to me about *Rainbow Swash* is the scale of its apparent imperfection—there's a lot of precisely imprecise detail at the edges of the enormous messy brush strokes (the opposite of lapidary, which interests me equally). Challenges to everyday human scale confuse me.

Driving north from Boston, the first signs of the New Hampshire border are the giant tax-free Stateline Liquor stores and the highway route numbers encased in the shape of the Old Man of the Mountain. Before I first saw the actual rock formation I expected it to be huge, given the scale of its local fame, but the series of granite ledges that formed the Old Man's profile was so relatively small and high up the side of a mountain that from the viewing point on Interstate 93 the figure was difficult to see and remarkably underwhelming. I wanted the face to be of Rushmore-sized proportions, and yet it was so perfectly representative of small-scale New England and its subtle wonders. Still, the presence of a face was unquestionable, its craggy features underscored by an angular stone beard. The first known sighting of the Old Man was by surveyors in 1805, and it quickly became a symbol of the hardscrabble lives and Puritan values of much of the local population (well, maybe I'm extrapolating, but to me it's symbolic of those things. You wouldn't find such a big deal made of it in any other state). In 1945 the formation was designated the state emblem and it made its first appearance on the license plate and highway route signs. Ten years later it gained its own US postage stamp.

But by the time the Old Man was first spotted (or known to be spotted, by white people), millennia of freezing and thawing had already taken a toll on the formation. Fissures opened and spread rapidly through the head. That of all the potential rock visages in all the world, this so-recently-adopted state treasure was so seriously structurally compromised is wonderful to me—eons and all of human time compressed into decades. In the 1920s they began shoring it up, first with chains, then later with cement, steel rods, protective plastic covering and a gutter to divert damaging runoff. Despite all this cheating of nature, the structure finally collapsed in 2003. Mourners piled flowers at the cliff's base, and an Old Man of the Mountain Memorial is now underway.

The idea was eventually rejected, but a significant contingent wanted to adhere a full-size synthetic replica of the Old Man to the side of the mountain. Instead, you can now pay to view its former outline superimposed on the mountain through coin-operated viewfinders. With the naked eye you see only sheer glacial escarpment, the Old Man's features completely fallen from the face.

I spent a lot of time in New Hampshire growing up, at summer camp and on weekends at the house of a family friend who is a granddaughter of Grover Cleveland. The rambling, ramshackle house, called Intermont, was one of Cleveland's summer homes. There were a lot of dusty museum-worthy objects lying around, like Grover's wooden fishing rods and his wire-rim reading glasses, which I liked to put on and try to read with. Outside, there was a latticed gazebo slowly collapsing under Concord grape vines. I recently had a madeleine moment when I ate a Concord grape for the first time in many years. The flavor is musty and redolent of a time when darker shades of flavor—anise and orange zest—were

more prevalent. It's the synesthetic taste of umber and ambergris—
further proof that taste, as in sensory predilection, can be dated.

Not long ago I read about a secret surgery Cleveland had during
his second term to remove a cancerous growth in his upper jaw. It
was a politically delicate time, apparently, amid a financial crisis
and heated debate about the efficacy of the gold standard, which
Cleveland fought to maintain. The operation was performed on a
private yacht in Long Island Sound in an effort to evade the press
and any questions about the President's health or capabilities.
A good chunk of his upper jaw was removed, resulting in some
facial deformity and speech difficulties, so he was later fitted with
a prosthetic rubber palate that restored his speech and appearance.
In spite of the efforts to keep the operation out of the news, the
story was soon leaked. Doctors claimed publicly that they were
merely extracting teeth.

The malignancy and metastatic potential of Cleveland's growth
were indeterminable at the time, and he wound up dying many
years later of other causes. I often think about how some kind
of cancer could be growing in my body at any moment without
my knowing it. I see seething CGI cells zoomed in on from the
cosmos of the body, like in the revelatory moment of a TV medical
drama. The cancer could be local, widespread, operable or incur-
able. I might have only a few years or weeks to live. In an instant,
select bits of everything I've ever known or done draw up to my
perennially potential diagnosis like metal filings around Wooly
Willy's chin. Un-bang of memory, five o'clock shadow on setting
face. Determined whiskers.

So much of our collective cultural memory radiates from Boston,
cleaving the land with fissures of history and their negative space.
But deep beneath the apparent assemblage of the city lie undocu-
mented remnants of other spatial arrangements. I have a hard time

swallowing that all of history's miscarried bits aren't somewhere collected, cataloged and available for me to sort through and piece together as I choose, into impractical placemats of broken Wedgwood, trysts, intentions and pheasant feathers. That not everything is or isn't and there you have it.

But information is selected for survival, and the indeterminate is its critical missing chromosome—the epistemological gold standard, a free-floating pince-nez. Have to free up your head face in order to catch it. Tête à tête à tête.

With her cancer diagnosis, Corita Kent was given six months. (Nowhere can I find what type of cancer she had. Was it some kind of unmentionable female variety? The internet is made of its holes.) She continued painting up to the very end, kicking the filings around, opening purple brackets. Now only the permanent possibility of the presence of Ho Chi Minh saves the swash, makes it an indigo stripe on a barber's pole, spiraling endlessly upwards in place.

Information is dead. What matters are the arrangements—I mean actively. I close your eyes, Cleveland, and put on your wavy glasses. They cast a diaphanous halo around us.

Between the unknown and the unknowable there's something to do with dinosaur bones. My three-year-old loves prehistory and outer space, and while I can't access his extemporary understanding of those places, I know I'd like to float there. If space is the shape of the universe, then there's room and a room for everything.

Specters have only relative extents. Physical and temporal scales are inversely proportionate. Some of the time. The work of leaf-eating ants. Glaciers slowly scratch figures into the earth, calve at the cracked, insupportable ends.

SLINGSHOT OUROBOROS

If there's a theme to my work, it's reflexivity. It's beyond reflexiv-ity. It's the trite-and-true self-self-reflexivity of standing between two mirrors, receding from and into one. Toward that end, which is not an end, but a perpetual process of self-digestion and evacu-ation, I often quote my own poems. It's a part of the hammering home ("a weary, insistent banging").

What I am trying to access, though, is not myself, but every-thing other than. I'm a slingshot Ouroboros ("I mean I'm a rebar Medusa") and my impetus is language. Thus, the images of pocking, peppering, punching through this self-healing wall that runs through and around my poems. And while the sledgehammer might not bring down the house, it can still put a decent hole in the drywall.

The sloggery is addictive. I swing the hammer again and again and again for the momentary thrill of poking through to the other side and getting a glimpse of the extra-linguistic conditions that might exist there—some kind of vestigial memory or form of perception that can't be caught with words. Whether it's a state more like presence or absence I can't say. But I have a sense that I can only get there by saying—exhausting myself via words, exhausting words.

The tricky thing, of course, is the wall is made of the rocks being shot at it. Word against word, bone to bone. John Henry's hammer made of mountains. We're all doing it—doing what we're doing while talking about doing it and here I am in so many words. Jabbing my pen-extended-finger not at something that can't be described, but at my faith in the existence of what can't be de-scribed. I'm not entirely clear what it is I'm not describing, but I've described it as the brief bouts of weightlessness in parabolic flight.

While the topics I take on in my work are diverse, the whole writing endeavor feels of a piece and each individual poem or work but a version of an only indirectly effable set of conditions or sensibilities. The conditions might be fundamental or not and may or may not actually exist. Maybe I just want them to. There's no baseline version of what I'm stabbing at—all versions are only relative to and moving away from one another, like dots on an inflating balloon. With each I try to mortally puncture the surface, but the holes heal up, become, at best, niggling paper cuts. My religious hope is to one day effect a compound fracture with the aggregate.

I always think about the 2004 film *The Notebook*. It's narrated as a series of flashbacks onto the drawn-out, dramatic courtship of a beautiful young couple during the 1940s. The intermittent present-day scenes take place in a nursing home, where an older man reads a diary containing the love story to an older woman who has lost her memory. She is entertained by the story, but not sure why it's being read to her.

The film's conceit, which isn't revealed until toward the end, is that, of course, this is the elderly woman's own diary, and this man is her one-time lover, longtime husband and father of her children. Over and over again, he reads her own account of their love story to her until she has a momentary breakthrough of lucidity wherein she remembers who he is, then they slow-dance together until she forgets again, starts screaming, and is hauled back to her room for more meds. The ending has them die together in one another's arms.

As an ars-poetic envelope, the "breaking through to lucidity" cliché feels useful. If it's soap-operatic, so be it—the action is dramatic. Those moments of euphoric clarity that writing induces are what I live for ("I mean the moment / a woman exhales / and slides beneath / her mounds of bubbles"). I feel shame for making these references, but maybe cheapness is a way through the wall. *The Notebook* is notorious for inducing weeping (yes, I did), and if I could put my finger on and employ in writing what it is, exactly, that unlooses the mind and adheres the body to what is the matter, then I could happily die in my own arms.

While each puncture wound I inflict on the retaining wall of my consciousness heals, beginning again doesn't feel like Sisyphusian drudgery. Maybe it's a matter of practice, by which I don't mean that writing myself out of the word-bound world gets easier each time, but that I have a clearer sense of where it is I'm trying to get to, even if the parameters of that place are no more clear. The floating just feels more right with each parabolic nosedive.

The scale of language is human, and humans do not exist on a comprehensive scale.

"I will die with this hammer in my hand." Swinging at the mountain, my own image chiseled into it. We finish each other's sentences, me and this thing I'm slow-dancing with.

THE NEEDLE

In 2005, Rusty and I spent our first wedding anniversary in a Central California beach town called Cayucos. After dinner one night we wound up at a dingy bar, where we sat next to a man who told us he was a Clamper. We didn't know what that was, but it explained the traffic-style signs on the walls that read things like "Clamper Crossing."

The man was drunk. He tried to explain what a Clamper was and we gleaned he was part of a thuggish fraternal organization. The members were motorcycle enthusiasts and had a mission to protect widows and children—the children part seemed genuine, the widows part, gross. Their other mission, he told us, was to preserve the history of the American West, although he didn't seem all that clear on how it was done.

The online record of the Clampers' history is garbled (both intentionally and not), but I now know that the organization's official name is E Clampus Vitus, which is nonsense Latin for something lively whose nineteenth-century humor I can't access. It was founded during the Gold Rush and, in contrast with the earnest rituals of other esoteric fraternal orders, like the Elks and Masons, it subsists on the ridiculous and inside jokes. The group's motto is *Credo Quia Absurdum,* which is shortened from the Latin for "I believe because it is absurd." Tellingly, Mark Twain was one of the organization's most famous members. In more recent years, it's become a biker fraternity and drinking club with a fuzzy relationship to its origins. It does some charitable fundraising and also mounts and dedicates plaques to lesser-known historical sites and events, which is its contribution to preserving Western heritage. Most of the plaques memorialize oddball Gold-Rush-era incidents and characters, and some are of inscrutable significance. The text is often excessively long and badly in need of editing:

MADERA ZOO

IN THE YEAR 1912 A MR. WILLIAM KING HEISKELL
BUILT AN AVIARY WITH ITS FIRST INHABITANTS
BEING A GREEN PARROT AND SEVERAL SPECIES OF
BIRDS FROM AROUND THE WORLD.

THE ZOO ALSO HAD SEVERAL PONDS AND WATER
FOUNTAINS AND A BANDSTAND.

ALTHOUGH THE MADERA ZOO WASN'T FULL OF
MANY SPECIES OF ANIMALS, THERE ARE SEVERAL
STORIES ABOUT A FAMOUS PARROT NAMED 'POLLY'
AND A ALLIGATOR NAMED 'GALAHAD.' POLLY WAS
MOST POPULAR FOR HIS COLORFUL VOCABULARY
THAT HE LEARNED FROM HIS MINER FRIENDS AND
HIS ABILITY TO MIMIC THEM.

GALAHAD — A NINE-FOOT ALLIGATOR SPENT MOST
OF HIS EARLY YEARS IN A SMALL BATHTUB BEHIND
A SALOON OWNED BY A MR. GLASS WHO USED TO
KID WITH THE CHINESE AND THEM THAT HE WAS
ACTUALLY A LITTLE CHINESE DRAGON.

POLLY NEARLY MET HIS DEMISE WHEN HE AND AN-
OTHER OCCUPANT OF THE PARK (A RACOON) HAD
ENCOUNTERED EACH OTHER AND THE RACOON'S
INTENTION WAS TO HAVE POLLY FOR DINNER THE
RACOON WAS BANISHED FROM THE PARK AND POLLY
LIVED HIS REMAINING YEARS WITH MR. HEISKELL'S
DAUGHTER.

AFTER HIS DEATH HE WAS SENT TO A TAXIDERMIST,
STUFFED AND RESIDES IN THE PRESENT COURT-
HOUSE MUSEUM.

DEDICATED BY E CLAMPUS VITUS
GRUB GULCH CHAPTER 41-49
AUGUST 11 2007.

These plaques throw the generally accepted relativity of human
events' scales and significance out of whack. They're like dialog

boxes popping out from the desert, the negative space of the painting, superseding the seeming blankness of the landscape and the canvas. California is conducive to these geometric shenanigans, with its vast spaces and endless embodiments of the sublime that defy you to locate individual events within them. Here in the Northeast, the close quarters, lower sky and insistent textbook claims on the terrain can make attempts at landscape reclamation fizzle. Historic plaques are closely packed and even the vast swathes of deciduous woods seem full of themselves and antithetical to such open gestures as earthworks.

I appreciate the Clampers' arbitrary approach to relocating the foci of human history. A phenomenon that I refer to repeatedly in my work, and which now undergirds my own approach to apprehending the world, is that optical illusion with the white grid on a black field. At the lines' intersections you see fuzzy gray dots, but only out of the corner of your eye. When you try to look directly at them they disappear, and then pop back up in the periphery of your vision. To me, those dots represent extra-linguistic, contrapuntal possibilities for comprehending existence, and, paradoxically, I use language to try to focus on them for a moment. I can't quite resolve the dots or linger on them long enough to clearly define their nature, but the grid is political, historical, and my eye and its corner are largely defined by gender and economics. The dots are made of all of these things at once and something much more, in addition to else. The natural world and the conditions of place are both inside and all around. (I want to say "so there".)

I don't know if it's possible to break or break out of the grid lines' framework, but you can dig around in the squares of space it contains. Think of a formal French garden, the intersections of its stiff box-lined walkways celebrated with looming statues of war heroes. Now think of the earthworms navigating and tunneling around the paths and parterres. I mean there.

OCCASIONAL MONUMENT
"In Budapest, a necropolis of shifting foci grid-dots, Soviet heroes, missing limbs."

The Clampers' plaques outsize the importance of small events and deeds, in contrast with the civic practice of trying to encapsulate both the individual and collective suffering of scores of people by funneling them all into one comparatively slight physical instant. War and disaster memorials' lists of names intend both to create a poignantly generalized blur and to elicit the specificity of each individual's experience, but they tend to just become themselves and their own physical manifestations as self-referential memento mori—a reminder of their own death-by-definition. Same with cemeteries. I found both Arlington and Normandy agitating, and not in the way I'm supposed to.

It's not the jingoism but the manipulative grandeur that gets me, the quantity-over-quality assessment of suffering. It is necessary that they exist, however, even if only to display their own insufficiency. Maybe the insufficiency itself is the true monument to humanness, an open question.

OCCASIONAL FROTTAGE MONUMENT
A terracotta army of more than 8,000 soldiers to protect me in my real life. I mean a copy of the one that already exists. This is a work on paper.

What kind of gesture could possibly capture the simultaneously outsized and infinitesimal scale of a human life? The Clampers' plaques make me wonder if only the absurd can. Absurdity is a palliative to insufficiency. And it's about time. Time slows, slides up its skirt and flashes its man hours. Absurdity graphs its own labor against time and shows the two to be in wild disproportion, saying on behalf of its perpetrator, yes, this archness is how I choose to consume my moments. Consider the artist Tom Friedman, who created a sculpture of approximately 3,000 garbage bags meticulously layered one inside the other. Another piece features a roll of toilet paper that he unrolled, removed the tube from, and then flawlessly re-rolled with perfectly aligned edges and no discernible space at the center. His work is perfectly futile and perfectly memorious, evoking the body of the artist laboring in lumbering real time, pursuing sublimely banal perfections.

Maya Lin once described her subterranean black gash of a Vietnam veteran's memorial as a "wound"—the object of a wounding. In a 1994 documentary she talks about how she first researches a site and its history and comes to a verbal understanding of its significance before even visiting the physical place. I don't know, but would guess that many landscape architects and artists would claim to privilege their intuition by visiting a site first and having it "tell them" what it wanted before doing in-depth historical research. The way I write poems is that chicken and that egg at the same time. The writing comes from the body and the mind and the site. I want it to occupy a physical space, to make divots in the desert. To wound. By its two-dimensional definition, I can't make it do that, but there is a muscular meaning at inception—I hold my breath, overarch my back. Feel the edge of my chair and the floor, pressing.

OCCASIONAL ASPIRATIONAL MONUMENT
BAG OF WIND (CHOKE ON YOUR OWN)

It's funny and makes sense that the respective heydays of earthworks and conceptual art were virtually simultaneous. Yoko Ono's *Grapefruit* came out only four years before Robert Smithson's foundational essay, "The Sedimentation of the Mind: Earth Projects." It's as though the representative capabilities of tools suited to the scale of the human world had been exhausted, so artists were reaching for something extra-human ("extra" meaning both "more than" and "more of"). Earthworks and conceptual art are opposites in so many ways—one quintessentially material, the other equally immaterial—but both are absurd and insufficient in their comprehensive inaccessibility and resistance to containment in a frame. I want these qualities in writing. I reach for outsized physicality to a degree that only theory can satisfy, and only in theory. So I continually find myself describing what it is that I'm trying to do while trying to do it and also make it huge.

OCCASIONAL CONCEPTUAL MONUMENT
Don't read what I write. Grind it beneath your heel, like glass. Sweep up the sharp dust and stick it in your eye. Bleed until complete.

We are in possession of a hideous nativity scene. Rusty remembers it as a fixture of his childhood Christmases, so when my in-laws were downsizing and distributing their belongings, he particularly wanted it. The figures are large and, even he admits, terribly ugly, so the set remains in the basement. It seems we can't get rid of it, even though we don't display it.

Why does merely remembering something make it meaningful? And why isn't the memory itself sufficient? Cognitive science suggests that each time we remember something we are really just recalling the last time we remembered it, over time distorting and rewriting what we think of as our most fundamental experiences. Each memory becomes only its forever modulating self, pulling away from the original context and blowing up in relative pro-portion with each visitation. Time grows a bulging cul-de-sac to accommodate it.

Our memories are rubbings of rubbings of our wishful anticipatory epitaphs. We might be made of our memories, but we think we are made of our inscriptions. Inscription is a stand-in for absence, which it tries to represent as the negative space of presence, like glinting marble chips falling around the figure. But absence is not anti-presence—it is only itself.

OCCASIONAL REMINDER MONUMENT
NEVER TAKE PICTURES. LEAVE ONLY FOOTPRINTS (TO FILL).

In November 2012 a factory fire in Bangladesh took the lives of 112 garment workers. They were sewing hoods onto sweatshirts for huge international brands whose higher-ups claimed either that they never knew this particular factory was in their employ or that they had explicitly forbidden working with it because of the facility's disregard of fire codes and worker welfare. I read the story in the *NY Times* and what most struck me about it was how small and remote the suffering of the mostly anonymous victims seemed as measured against the scale of global capitalism and the materiality of its countless mundane products. Faces pressed against window grilles do not a high-profile disaster make.

Does some pain mean more than other pain?

A baby is born and left to die on an open plain. It has a name, but doesn't know it.

Pain is a fuzzy gray dot with definite dimensions that can't be measured, except on a personal scale. Hospital nurses will ask you to rate your pain from one to ten before administering medication. This task is difficult for me. Am I ranking my pain against itself or against all other pain I've experienced? I'm fortunate to have only ever been hospitalized during and while recovering from childbirth. Both times I felt the pain of labor and childbirth itself to be very lonely, and I can't explain why this is. It goes against my desolate sense that if pain has meaning, it has to do with the extent to which it is witnessed. Surely the experience of giving birth to a child is one of the most painful. Surely being born is another. But while mother and child simultaneously, symbiotically suffer and witness, neither knows nor thinks of the other's pain, and maybe that's what makes it so lonely—it's a pain mutually witnessed and mutually unheeded by two entwined people, the physical part of whose attachment is but a taste of the crushing, comprehensive conjoinment to come.

If witness makes pain mean, so might remembering—memory makes you your own ongoing witness. But one can neither remember the pain of one's own birth nor call back the pain of childbirth.* And while the pain of childbirth is to be dreaded, it does not matter so long as it's behind you, even if you want it to. Why is it that the memory of one's own physical suffering is not usually troubling, but the anticipation of future suffering is? And yet, knowing that a loved one has suffered before death is terrible. But knowing that a loved one has suffered and then survived is not very terrible at all. In any case, one is not suffering now.

An unnamed baby is born and left to die on an open plain. (You little black hole.) (Shut up.)

With or without a witness or a body's name, I have to believe that suffering takes up space, that it's somewhere recorded and stored. That there's a mark or memorial wormhole for each of us in the positive or negative space of space. The dark matter of two faces or

---

* although it seems to me I can usually recall the sensation of mental pain, including that tunneled-in forlornness of being in labor. Or of milk letdown. Or of being hung over. It's as though the utter realization of the body makes the mind disengage. But is the disengagement a retreat or a plunge into freedom from everything that is not oneself? I wish I knew how to pay more attention.

a vase.

OCCASIONAL NOSTALGIA MONUMENT

AN ACTUAL PLAYER-PIANO SCROLL, MUSIC MADE OF HOLES.

The Museum of Jurassic Technology in Los Angeles is often
likened to a cabinet of curiosities, the collection of oddities and
natural wonders assembled by wealthy late-Renaissance Euro-
peans. Among other phenomena, the museum houses the microminiature sculptures of Hagop Sandaldjian, which are so small
that they are displayed under magnifying lenses. Born in Egypt
in 1931, the artist trained as a violinist in Moscow and Armenia.
In the 1960s his rigorous study and obsessive practice led him to
develop a musical technique based on ergonomics, which lever-
aged the muscular force of the musician against the external force
of gravity and the mechanics of the instrument, ideally making the
instrument an extension of the body working with, and in counter-
point to, the physical world.

One of Sandaldjian's students introduced him to the world of
microminiature sculpture and he soon applied himself and his
ergonomic theory to creating artworks that fit inside the eye of a
small needle or balance on a bisected human hair. Working with
a microscope, he learned to time his minute creative gestures between heartbeats, since his pulse was capable of compromising his
precision. He crafted his pieces from lint and dust motes, which he
manipulated with precise homemade tools such as needles tipped
with diamond dust. He even painted his sculptures with brushes
made from sharpened strands of hair. His miniatures' details can't
be seen without magnification, and their fuzzy blown-up outlines
foreground the mechanics and parameters of your vision.

Sandaldjian's sculptures each took as long as fourteen months to complete (by contrast, Smithson's *Spiral Jetty* took just six days to build.) The miniatures' screaming diseconomies of scale are just part of what makes them so touching. The thing that takes them beyond the oddly obsessive into the realm of the wonderful and mysterious is the insipidness of the imagery. Many of the pieces are brightly painted Disney figures—Goofy atop a needle's eye, Snow White and the Seven Dwarves lined up along a spliced hair. That anti-expressive, self-abasing devotion to rendering cartoon figures creates a counter-sublimity, a non-non-site of self or singularity that shuts you up like a telescope (to quote Alice, whose adventures in inhuman scale are also insipid from overuse, but exactly what I mean. All the time).

It might be that this kind of seeming mere curiosity makes the best monument of all—the oddity happening in the periphery of your purview. Like Tom Friedman's sculptures and the Clampers' eccentric commemorative gestures, Sandaljian's artworks are a kind of living anti-statuary. They are monuments in and to time itself, rather than attempts to capture particular instances of it, and that is what keeps them alive. A defining element of living is change, and so change is necessary to an eternally evocative monument. By nature, a curiosity remains curious, refuses to resolve into its raison d'être. It defies adaptation with its adhesion to the moving body that made it and elicits an ongoing wonder at the perceived boldness or inanity of the maker's commitment or indifference to time consumption. Like a fuzzy gray dot, it can't be pinned down, sized up or located. It is slight. It is niggling. It is moving.

OCCASIONAL MAKER'S MONUMENT

ALL THE RIGHT TOOLS MUST BE HARDER THAN THE MEDIUM.

To lunge at the finish of this strung-out syllogism, since the body is a vessel of change and anything inhering to it is a thing in flux, a sense of the body that made the work (and by "work" I mean both process and product) is necessary to living, moving, unresolvable art. The body and the work must be of a piece—beating, blinking, circulating, wearing themselves out and using themselves up. In paradoxical perpetuity. And differently each time. How, I don't know. I'm nearly exhausted.

Imagine an arrow hurtling straight from the hand of the body and then lodging, forever trembling, in the work. The impetus remains manifest. I want to call this relationship "ergonomic," but that's not accurate, exactly, since I don't necessarily or always mean with a sense of efficiency. Rather than a surgeon with her scalpel, I see the artist staggering around under the weight and force of the chainsaw, cutting into the coffee table, getting in an occasional whack at the man-sized block of marble. It's a necessary sense of the body that makes the work in time, of the tools of representation as a mere and palpable and perfect medium. Of the heartbeat or the diastole in the form or the line or the rigid stack of garbage bags. The body and the wound at once, at the moment.

> make the whole world
> a monument to you

My conceptual conviction.

The question remains: how to write curiosities, bodied monuments of words that can't be apprehended, that flicker for an instant in the margins of the mind, and then reappear elsewhere, changing all of the contextual terms with each visitation, perpetually occasional.

Words are enormous containers, and yet they hold so little. The trick is to lug and arrange them in such a way as to yield the smallest units of perception, i.e., poetry. Poetry is absurd. Poetry is sufficiently momentary, the telescope collapsing with a *snap*. (Watch your fingers.) The long-range seeing part is relatively easy—the struggle is in the collapsing, the better half of the poem's purpose. The struggle is also the poem. And then: is it two faces or a vase?

PERPETUAL OCCASIONAL MONUMENT
I MEAN I MEAN I MEAN

I want a new memory. Running over trips and incidents in my head, all I remember is their self-supplanting palimpsests. I need triggers, but they have to find me, like the objects and moments in the day that suddenly bring back last night's dream. And the triggers, for the most part, live with other people. There are hundreds of people who can remember things about me that I cannot. Small, incorporeal memorials to me move over the globe, flickering like fuzzy dots. Imagine a map of everyone who remembers you, the dots disappearing and new ones cropping up for as long as you keep on meeting people. And then, after you are gone, they snuff out one by one.

One week before flying back east to be married, Rusty and I were driving on the hot infrequently traveled road that heads inland from Mendocino and ends at the 101 in Ukiah, California. Somewhere in the middle we stopped at the side of the road to pee. I had just crouched down behind a boulder when I heard a loud rattle beneath me. Millimeters from my flip-flop a fat black rattlesnake was coiled, its head reared and looking at me. At the same time as I screamed and did my best to run with my pants around my ankles, the snake took off into the brush. I think about this incident all the time—it's one of my favorite stories. But how many more times will I remember it? That element of ontological mystery about something that feels so close to me is the crease that collapses me into myself.

RING ROAD

I write a lot about place. And from it to the extent that I can. I know I'm really in it when I hear the feedback looping out from and back into my head. But these moments of utter occupation are hard-won because place flickers and moves from beneath you, like a fuzzy gray dot at the intersections of a black-and-white grid. Just when you get there it's gone to the corner of your eye.

One way that I try to get at place is through its people. For the last year or so I've been collecting components for a project about Isabella Stewart Gardner and her eponymous museum in Boston. The museum is located on the Fenway, the first in a series of city parks designed by Frederick Law Olmsted and known as the Emerald Necklace. The museum opened in 1903 and was designed by Gardner herself in the style of a 15th-century Venetian palazzo that she flipped inside-out—the cold, hard facade contains its opulent interior like a geode. Tiers of Italianate balconies and arched windows rise around a skylit courtyard filled with palms, fountains and Roman statues. The galleries are lit low like private rooms and layered with plunder—tapestries, fireplaces, altarpieces, antique furnishings, gilded ceilings, wall coverings and stained-glass windows that Gardner obsessively collected during her world travels. The outermost layer consists of her vast art collection, works ranging from Titian to Degas to Whistler.

Each room is jam-packed and just-so. There is a sense of completion to her arrangements that makes isolating and contemplating any one element difficult and disruptive. She imposes her contextual constraints on annunciations, pietas and Vermeer's belabored attempts at perspective, damping the works' resonance, bending their associative trajectories around into the ring road of the city of herself. Her motto, *C'est mon Plaisir*, ripples beneath a phoenix on the museum's emblem.

Gardner tried to hermetically seal her world by making it a condition of its bequest to the city nearly 100 years ago that no element or artwork ever be added, removed or moved from its place in the museum. Nonetheless, there are leakages. In the second-floor Dutch Room a self-portrait of Rembrandt in a feathered cap faces a blank space on the opposite wall where the painter's *Storm on the Sea of Galilee* used to be. In 1990 thieves made off with an estimated $500 million in artworks and objects that have not been recovered. The spaces create an imbalance in those rooms—they gape and swallow your eye. But because of Gardner's rigid stipulation, the art can't be rearranged to fill them.

The museum is a large-scale, lifelong installation project, whose self-containment deeply satisfies what a friend once called my "completist panic," a condition that I've since realized is the leading impetus for all of my work (not to mention the greatest source of my frustration with raising two small children). The exhausting availability of information and the speed at which it continually shifts and flattens the perceptual landscape of our cultural present makes me want to zip myself into Gardner's close round world. I can breathe my own air there, smell my own breath. And yet, even though they endlessly debate and explain loopholes into it, the museum board and staff mostly continue to obey Gardner's stricture, and so the stolen artworks broadcast their own punctures in her project. This dos-à-dos-à-dos of perfection, its theoretical impossibility and actual undoing, is what consumes me.

I recently gave a reading with Susan Howe, whom I'm often compared to because of our common interest in the early history of New England. To writers of other origins New England is a brand, and with good reason—the depth, intensity and entrenchment of its borrowed lyric tradition make for a lot to lug around and plug yourself into if you choose. I think of the locus of my work both as a place among many others and as a challenge because of its particular baggage. But it is first and foremost the place that means me and that I mean to mean back. This reciprocity is what Howe and I have in common. After the reading she told me that she is also working on a project about Isabella Stewart Gardner.

In *Civilization and its Discontents*, Freud compares the human mind to a city with all of its ancient and modern structures simultaneously intact and available: "...the observer would need merely to shift the focus of his eyes, perhaps, or change his position, in order to call up a view of one or the other." In *The Midnight*, Howe writes, "In relation to detail every first scrap of memory survives in sleep or insanity." In both cases the fine points of memory are theoretically accessible, but there is a fundamental difference in how they are accessed. Freud's mind-place is an impossible palimpsest of static, equally extant layers. Howe embodies hers in her tireless multimania, only her place is made in the process of breaking into it, so details are intermittently available and always recombining, swallowing each other up and changing the view in a dynamic vat of past and present. While Freud's conceptualization of the mind is utterly subjective, Howe's is of a piece with the world—it is inextricably bound up with history. But she removes the connective tissue of the historical record and lets the past's clippings, offal and picked bones lie looking like themselves and the minds that left them there. If Freud's mind is a perfectly preserved place with actual parameters, Howe's borderless place is made of fractured ruins of many minds and memories that run away like grid-dots as you get near them.

Like Freud's wishful vision of mind and memory as discrete artifact, Gardner's project fails both because and in spite of her great effort to keep her collection intact and impervious to change. Howe, on the other hand, works just as hard to undo what she's doing at the same time as she's doing it—while she acts on the urge for completion with her rigorous work, the work is always its own product. It's a pilgrim's continuous progress toward where she already is and what she already knows, but with a resulting deeper understanding of why she knows it. With collage and visual components she introduces chance and dimensions of subjectivity that deepen and soften her field of inquiry, allowing her searching roots to push further.

The Midnight is patched together from pieces of and reminiscences related to old books, poets, historical figures and Howe's mother, the Irish actress Mary Manning. One of its more prominent themes is the history of bed hangings, curtains that were once draped around beds in order to keep certain things out (cold, ghosts, prying eyes) and other things in (heat, noise and nebulous qualities of sleep). Other than a grave, the place where one sleeps is as local as it gets. It's a location to which one gives oneself over. Sleep is a state of being both fully present and realized, and also absent, and mere witness to oneself, where one's endlessly combinatoric fragments are called forth in inscrutable relationships. *The Midnight* exists in such a roughly woven dreamplace with the warp of time removed. Picking through and heaping up the weft, Howe never presumes comprehension or comprehensiveness: "Thinking is willing you are wild / to the weave not to material itself."

And yet, "Non-connection is itself distinct / connection," and neither does Howe prevent patterns from forming. But when she suggests or allows a connection, she makes sure to point out her own hand in the sleight, the "intersection of realities" she sets up, leaving room for the reader to call out the contrivance. The intersection remains nonetheless. In the course of the book a thread of performance emerges, binding Mary Manning to *A Midsummer Night's Dream*, Jonathan Edwards, Japanese Noh, and Howe's own visit to Harvard's library to research Emily Dickinson wherein her consciousness of her attire and its loud signaling threaten to subsume her purpose in being there. Curtains contain both the bed and the stage. Amtrak makes a number of stops along the way, bringing her places together—and/or choosing them—including Howe's current home of Guilford, CT, where the train's whistle keeps her awake at night. (Olmsted describes a childhood sojourn in Guilford during his own bout of insomnia.) But just as you begin to give in to the shapely web of connections, she drops a reminder that "little relocated facts epistemically relocated tell very little". This struggle between binding and rending and the difficult work of doing both and neither is the tensile strength of her project.

Howe manifests sleeplessness, indulges the desire for exhaustiveness while demonstrating its futility. She enacts the maxim of her fellow re-visioners of New England, delivering content by the bucket-load and letting form be taken. Isabella Stewart Gardner, on the other hand, says, "That is enough." In her impervious sphere, form and content complete one another like a call and response to prayer. So, what will Howe do with Isabella? I see her dropping a microphone into the depths contained by the empty frames on the wall and recording what she hears there. Those gaps are the cataracts in—and the chance to escape from—Isabella's circumscribed vision. While I am interested in the premises and attempted hermeticism of the vision itself, Howe is holding her listening glass to the chinks. But we are both Rembrandt boring holes into his missing masterpiece, the beautiful thing we know we could make if we would only stop unpainting it. Our parallels derail themselves, their vanishing point a maw.

* * *

I was born in Boston and grew up 20 minutes away in Wayland, Massachusetts. To get there you take the Mass Pike to Route 128, the city's ring road, whose formal name is the Yankee Division

Highway. Drive north about two miles, take Exit 26 and follow the Post Road to the town center. Growing up I was within biking distance of Walden Pond, The Wayside Inn, the Alcotts' Orchard House and the Concord battlefield. My grandmother frequently took me and my brother on picnics at what's known locally as the Rude Bridge, thanks to Emerson's dedication, which it bears on a plaque at one end. There is a small visitors' center at which you can try on mobcaps and three-cornered hats.

At the center of this classic factual New England landscape was my family, which is of the traditional congregational sort. You talk about anything but what you're talking about, then have a few cocktails and forget both. Textbook Puritan derivatives, my relations tend to be parsimonious to the extreme, so they don't waste a lot of time on the tangle of human psychology. This innate economy manifests in a practical anti-parsimony principle when it comes to the material, where time is infinite and resources are discrete. When my great aunt Dodie died, found in her decrepit Providence manor house was a box labeled, "Pieces of String Too Small to Be Useful." My parents will drive thirty minutes from home for wholesale groceries. I joke they'd drive fifty miles for cheaper gas. I've gained from them these horn-locked notions that time is precious but can't confer advantage because we are all in it.

This is one version of the original Puritan paradox of hard work versus predestination that a dispositional New Englander some-how ignores, or reconciles and lives with. But I'm at odds, as a would-be completist who feels the press of time like a bundling board. I explore this perpetual state of emergency by doing my best to divide things down to their essence, even though I'll never get there. And I try to include everything and also different kinds of it, in addition to every bit of it. All the time. Every end of string. My poetic practice has shaped itself accordingly around Zeno's and Kant's paradoxical state of kinetic suspension—I want but can't have it all, so I keep to my place and divide mitotically.

Place is what clings most closely to the body that is not the body itself. For me, writing about where I've been and where I live is both an indulgence and a form of resistance—I can voraciously parse my own impetuses while thwarting my yen for hermeticism. I love to close loops but stop believing in them as soon as I do. In place and its attendant events there is always more to excavate and to try to synthesize. The ground keeps deepening and dividing beneath my feet.

* * *

After 11 years in San Francisco, Rusty and I moved to Providence in 2007. If space is what the body displaces and place is what it occupies, then I'd been beside myself, taking up space for over a decade. California's high sky and unbounded landscapes pulled me out of my own brain and body and the delimited conditions under which I was born and became myself. The removal gave me contrast in abundance. It also made my mind feel more perceptibly mechanical, like my synapses had grown and their firings slowed. But while this sense of relativity was exhilarating, in time it began to feel like a never-ending spacewalk. After a few years of floating I started pulling myself back in, writing increasingly about New England and using description to put me in my body there:

> The summer I was seven, the gypsy
> moths infested, caterpillars wriggled
> from the sky, tangled in my ratty
> hair, formed knots, crawling skin,
> shivers, peristaltic on the sidewalk.
>
> Stinging nettles, tiny hairs
> of hooked skin, throwing

burrs at others' backs, sticks
stabbing though your thin shirt

—Unbecoming Behavior

In the year before we moved back, I wrote *Unbecoming Behavior*,
which is about expatriatism and physical displacement—my own
and that of the writer Jane Bowles. It was an exploration of the
removal from a home and an experiment in remotely accessing
it. One way I tried to reinhabit Massachusetts was by evoking its
particular locating discomforts, especially the sticky summer heat
that California lacks. I wanted to swell and itch.

hives	buzz
at night	induced
by heat	pocked skin
throbbing	cicadas
shrieking	bites
the night	the glowing

bug zapper

From 3,000 miles away I stabbed at my "You Are Here" dot,
counting on never quite getting there lest it disappear or I adapt to
it. I needed to stay suspended somewhere just in front of it in order
to maintain the contrast necessary to think. And so moving back
east was fraught—I worried that I wouldn't be able to write there.
What I've since realized is that "there" was a place of my own
making and different from "here." Here is where I am, no matter
where and where else I'm pointing at.

* * *

From Wayland, return to 128, drive south one mile to Exit 25 in Weston and get on the Mass Pike. About 75 miles west is the Quabbin Reservoir visitors' center in Belchertown. (Due to the proximity of Athol, my uncle used to refer to this region as the "digestive tract of Massachusetts." A map is a maw.) Most of Boston's water comes from Quabbin, which was built in the 1930s by damming the Swift River and drowning the valley. The residents of Enfield, Prescott, Dana and Greenwich were relocated and the buildings were razed. More than 6,000 gravesites were moved. The disincorporated towns no longer appear on the map, but their streets and stone walls are still there. Supposedly you can see them from the air or when the water level is low.

I wrote *The Return of the Native*, which is partly about Quabbin, after driving back across the country to Rhode Island. The book is named for Thomas Hardy's, which I read right before we left. The jarring shift of that move had me thinking about the abstract and unstable qualities of maps, as well as about their revision, appropriation and erasure—how Hardy drew his Wessex map on top of the real one, how Quabbin wiped out a chunk of the Massachusetts map while adding a significant feature to it, and how even after all that time living there I still pictured California as a place on the U.S. map. When I called my parents, say, I actually saw myself in the map with a phone to my ear. I didn't think about Massachusetts that way. Massachusetts made me think of the feeling of being in it, and that is what makes me native, maybe.

Maps are one way we locate ourselves, relatively. But if anyone knows how to locate his characters by giving you the feeling of being in a place, it's Hardy. Each novel is contained within a real place that Hardy makes and that functions as its own social petri dish. Together, his carefully wrought characters and landscapes evoke the genius loci of 19th-century rural England, a place that in its self-containment is remote from this highly mediated moment.

But rather than let them be, Hardy dulls and abstracts his places with a map, when the novels' respective settings don't even overlap and have little to do with the pseudonymous places to which they are retroactively assigned. London glares above the fake-medieval place names of Wessex like an over-bright and disorienting beacon.

Hardy was a completist and perhaps he panicked. It was not enough to have created a cluster of beautifully consummate things, he needed to bring them all together under an umbrella whose cheapness he either ignored or couldn't see. I retroactively assigned the chapter titles from Hardy's book to sections of my own *Return of the Native* in an approximation of the heavy load his map placed on his places. I was indulging the urge to undo what one has done well by trying to do more on top of or around it. While the titles forced narrative frames and a strong connection with Hardy onto my book, in most cases they also wound up feeling weirdly appropriate to their respective sections of the poem (and therewith swallowed the whole point in an analogous demonstration of cartographic peristalsis).

But if Hardy's map seems beside the point at best, other than as a brand, it does make me think about how one might merge relative and innate* qualities of place into a completely representational map depicting all of a place's factual and subjective history layered like innumerable vellum overhead-projector transparencies.†

I once explored this sort of experiential mapping in writing, in a Charles-Ives-esque long poem I've since retired, which, among other things, I stuffed with bits of songs and hymns and American folklore. About it, I once wrote, "If these walls could talk they'd

---

* I mean innate for each person—things both adherent and inherent to place. Just don't ask me which is which.

† I worry it's starting to look like everything I mean is only the internet.

sound just like this."[*]

* * *

Conflicting perceptions of the world as built versus the world as received might be the defining conflict of New England self-identity—the original Yankee division. A Puritan insists on having it both ways and ignores the dissonance. A transcendentalist does the same. Emerson says in *Nature*, "Build your own world" and also "I become a transparent eyeball. I am nothing; I see all; the currents of the universal being circulate through me." But there is no room in the purview for the largesse of paradox. I wrote about Fruitlands because I was interested in the inability to act and move that an extreme philosophical position can induce. The inhabitants were so intent on receiving and refusing to intervene in the physical world that they nearly starved after only seven months together.

Puritanism, Transcendentalism and other utopic New England test-tube worlds—Hopedale, the Shakers, the domain of Sylvester Graham—were created under pressured laboratory conditions of a nation's short gestation and vast amount of amniotic space. The philosophical deadlock of action and reception inherent to all of them touches off panic in the completist—if both everything and nothing depend on me, then I'm stuck, suspended like Achilles, who not only can't get ahead, but can't move at all as space and time subdivide around him like an endlessly shuffling deck of cards. And yet it is not possible not to move and act and be in time, and this again might be what furnishes the tension in poetry—deconstruct versus "make it new"—"theory at war with phenomena" (*The Midnight*). As a locus of poetic struggle, New England makes

---

[*] They didn't.

sense.

* * *

Exit 29b off Route 128 puts you on Route 2 West, which passes through Concord on its way to Acton, childhood home of Robert Creeley. A book that I return to repeatedly is *Robert Creeley and the Genius of the American Commonplace,* the greater part of which, according to the jacket, consists of an "interactive biographical essay culled from conversations between the poet and Tom Clark." Creeley talks a lot about the enduring influence of the Puritans' ideological conflict on his upbringing as well as about the intrinsic physical qualities of his native place that helped him to work outside of—or freely within, at least—the terms of that paralyzing inconsistency.

> Think.
> Slowly. See
> The things around you,
>
> Taking place.
>
> —"Massachusetts"

As things are allowed to take their places—to adhere themselves there—place becomes a way to apprehend them. In regard to what Creeley considered an ideal location from which to observe and write, Tom Clark quotes him as saying, "It is where one feels an intimate association both with the ground under one's feet and with all that inhabits the place as condition." He doesn't write about woods and fields and houses, but those places loosely enfold his poems the way a lantern holds light. A word that Creeley uses frequently when describing where he came from and that is central to my thinking about the role of place in writing is "immanence."

Tom Clark: You've spoken of an enlivening presence you felt in the landscape, the local woods. There's a sort of allegorical or emblematic landscape also evoked in the hymnal, perhaps not dissimilar to the lyric landscape of your poetry—not the lush greens of classic pastoral, but a bare, stripped woods of winter, all light and shadow.

Robert Creeley: Yes ... the language of the hymns brings back for me that still small voice, that curious immanence. I *did* know it as some immanence, or qualification, in the sense of the physical staging of the place. A hushed evening, twilight, say—the physical terms were not just evocative, but like, say, the way water sounds.

The way water sounds. That embodiment of immanence, inscape, physical presence has propelled me through many a sticky moment in my work. When exhausted by subjectivity, I fold into the qualities of place and find a momentary objective center in what emanates from there.

> I see love and need you
> to hear it: listen,
> I did once love someone
> who told me that

> he and some other boys would climb onto a roof over Main Street and cast clam-baited hooks into the air, where the seagulls would catch and swallow them. The boys would then fly the gulls like kites over Main Street. The dying birds would have seen the harbor and returning trawlers, their compatriots swarming like flies over fish heads with eyes in them, fish tails, the dilapidated Manufactory

> *—Beauport*

Even if it is only a desperate throe of perspective, this panoramic quality is not something you'd find in Creeley. Clark describes Creeley's work as having the "fated limitation to a condition of sight without perspective." His flat affect has a cinematic *verité* anticipated by Emerson's transparent eyeball: "I am nothing; I see all." The condemnation to vision is ironic, given that Creeley had only one working eye and another made of glass. But if he lacks the mechanical perspective afforded by two working eyes, he's also spared the cognitive dissonance in the difference between what is seen with the right eye and the left that others' brains fuzz over. While his poems are *about* lack of perspective—collectively they feel like a struggle to escape from a sack—they are born of a stable place.

The perspective Creeley's poems are fighting for is denied by another kind of dissonance that refuses to resolve—the inadequacy of speech to express and thus facilitate understanding of the horrors of human existence. "Speech / is a mouth," gaping and flapping and always only uttering itself: "I think to say this / Wrongly." You get the sense in Creeley's poems that if only everything were effable then we might fruitfully assimilate it. He palpably, precisely manifests the dullness of words and the fumbling that we do with them, showing that meaning is possible in language, even if that meaning is another kind of its-own-mouth.

In my own fight for perspective, I keep trying to describe what achieving it feels like to me—weightlessness, punching through a self-healing wall, the screech of feedback. The success is momentary by nature because there's no permanent state of perspective to be had. Even the most sweeping prospect must accommodate pervasive change, but perspective also requires a vantage place. Susan Howe clips and collages the past into piles then climbs on top for a small view, drops microphones into cracks and calls up faint voices, digs deep into the bottomless hole of history in pursuit of her perspective. She works with the assiduousness of a Puritan. Creeley is more of a Transcendentalist, reclining in a sharp bed of pine needles. Howe writes *into* New England, Creeley writes *from* it. Neither tries to contain it. I try to contain it over and over again in fits and moments, like jars of fireflies jammed on the nightstand.

Howe's accretions resist closure in every possible way, including formally—whether she's working in series of tiny text boxes or swathes of prose, the work digs into and piles up on itself in a way that wants to go on forever. She makes heaps of scree, sometimes purposeful, sometimes accidental, and I can't think of anything she's written that wants to be beheld and admired discretely. Her writing to date feels continuous, but not contained. It is still building and splitting and smashing and sweeping itself up in new ways. She voices the immanence of history, which is as contingent and unclosed as a thing can be, since there are an infinite number of ways to organize it. And so her focus on New England is necessary—not the location itself, but the locatedness—because it allows her to keep drilling down toward the unreachable core and pull out more. She's done Jonathan Edwards over and over again but is still not done with him. Her work is to make more work for herself by unstitching time, one after nine.

Creeley's poems are formal objects to the utmost, but he never closes the loop of his exploration of subjectivity and language and the way they speak or don't speak to one another. Each poem is a whole but is also only one piece of conduit in an endless subjective plumbing project. It is also a clog, backing up all over itself in an almost defeatist reflexive maneuver. What allows him to have it both ways—open and contained—might be his terminal zingers, in which subject and object are the same, taking turns with the verb, as prepositions refuse to resolve into one way of meaning:

And all our nights be one, love
for all we knew.

— "Old Song"

We break things in pieces like
walls we break ourselves into
hearing them fall just to hear it.

— "The Answer"

One comes to a place he had not thought to,
looks ahead to whatever,
feels nothing lost but himself.

— "The day was gathered on
waking..."

Creeley's last lines resonate, but inwardly—the poem absorbs its
own vibrations. The poem is the mallet and the gong and the hand
that stops it.

* * *

Continue north on 128 and take Exit 26 to get to the Peabody-Es-
sex Museum in Salem (note: this is a different Exit 26 from the one
off which I grew up—128 is full of such loops for which to throw
you). When I was just starting to write poetry and looking for
a way to think about it, it was here that I encountered a Chinese
puzzle ball. Painstakingly carved by hand from a single piece of
ivory, a puzzle ball consists of nested concentric spheres of different symbolic motifs that move freely inside one another. By gently
manipulating the ball with a fine tool, the spheres' corresponding
holes can be lined up to allow you to see into the ball's center.

This seemed like a useful analogy. I could close my loops while nesting worlds within worlds interminably. The idea and its shape have stayed with me, from "the set of all sets that is a member of itself" in *Fruitlands* to the antique glass buoys that *Beauport's* Henry Sleeper collects:

> The small glass globes of purple, amber and blue are a solar system when the sun shines. Worlds orbit worlds and vanish into the rest of it when he squints through their empty centers.

While I want my poems to do and undo things both individually and collectively, creating a self-contained object does require some sort of closure of each poem's system. By nesting them and letting them reflect and refer back to one another incessantly I can have my terminal zingers and have them eat one another, too. These inter-referential relationships between the poems and me are facilitated by our common place.

* * *

Route 128 terminates in Gloucester, where I grew up spending summers and where my parents now live full-time. The city's perilous fishing trade and concomitant attraction for artists and writers helped to create the romantic New England sea trope that was once so central to American self-identification. Winslow Homer, Fitz Henry Lane, Kipling, Longfellow and T.S. Eliot depicted Gloucester fishermen at sea in iconic works suffused with salt, readymade for the canon. A local fishing shack has been the subject of so many quiet works of art it's known as Motif #1.

And yet Gloucester has kept tourists at arm's length and gentrification efforts often fail, so the place feels less self-conscious than many. It's that one-to-one relationship of the city to itself that makes artists want to depict it, which, in turn, has made it an artistically self-conscious place and one of poetry's zingiest locations. It is challenging to write about Gloucester, since it's a place that's at once extra "real," objectified and abstracted, and because someone has already written about it to the max. Charles Olson spread himself over it like plastic wrap. I admire his ambition, even if it didn't leave a lot of room for the rest of us. In the Maximus poems, he came as close to completing a project as might be possible or desirable, and the manifest tension between his push toward catalogic exhaustiveness and a metaphysical resistance to it influenced my own sense of what is impossible and undesirable in poetry.

Olson's solipsism bothers me, but please. Look at me. Still, there is a difference that I am still splitting into. Olson and I are both containers, although on different scales—he tried to encapsulate Gloucester in all its dynamism while I've tried to capture certain frozen moments of it. But we both poke holes in the bag, Olson with metaphysics and counter-colloquial cultural reference, me by creating and closing another container around it. The biggest difference in our projects might be one of ontological assumption— Olson's solipsism seems wishful and mine is fearful. I need there to be more, whereas he seems to hope and half-believe that he is enough. In either case, the innumerable points of entry into place provide an equal number of ways to triangulate back to the self.

***

While I'm still hovering toward exhaustiveness, I've learned to keep my place, whether it's where I come from or where I am. For now they're the same and I feel fortunate—as the locus of the original and fundamental American war with place, New England has a defining relationship to itself as a physical location. The first English settlers tried to harness it and the place resisted.

They learned to give in to the exigencies of the land at the same time as they continued to inscribe on and erase a whole other cultural conception of place from it. It is a place that was taken and then deliberately and dramatically made. Also, as the crucible of Anglo-American lyric tradition, New England is fertile ground for innovative appropriation. Howe, Creeley and Olson are my founding fathers of linguistic landscape architecture and I continue to consider my relationship to their place and respective places and my own place in them. I mean *consider* in the sidereal sense—to write like punching backlit holes through tin.

I regularly drive the length of 128 between Gloucester and Providence. My earliest colonial ancestors also lived and are buried here and this sense of original place gives me a specious but pleasing feeling of having returned to and arrived somewhere—of physical indivisibility and containment and home. If I never get out of here it won't be for lack of trying to stay.

Place is made and becomes itself. Autobiography is a dead end. But bloodlines do begin me at my body and for now this place means me, matters me, because I am in it.

Notes

REFERENCES

Page 87

"In Budapest…," Kate Colby, "Meridian," *Fruitlands* (Litmus Press, 2006), 45

Page 98

"In relation to detail…," Susan Howe, *The Midnight* (New Directions, 2003), 68

Page 99

"Thinking is willing you are wild to the weave…," *The Midnight*, 17

"Non-connection is itself distinct…," *The Midnight*, 17

"intersection of realities," *The Midnight*, 55

Page 100

"little relocated facts…," *The Midnight*, 134

Page 106

"theory at war with phenomena," *The Midnight*, 18

Page 107

"Massachusetts," *Selected Poems of Robert Creeley* (University of California Press, 1991), 188

Pages 107-108

Interview with Robert Creeley: Tom Clark, *Robert Creeley and the Genius of the American Commonplace* (New Directions, 1993), 41

Pages 108-109

"fated limitation to a condition of sight…," *Robert Creeley and the Genius of the American Commonplace*, 66

Page 109

"The Language," *Selected Poems of Robert Creeley*, 96

"The Whip," *Selected Poems of Robert Creeley*, 45

Page 111

"Old Song," *Selected Poems of Robert Creeley*, 9

"The Answer," *Selected Poems of Robert Creeley*, 109

"The day was gathered on waking…," *Selected Poems of Robert Creeley*, 178

ACKNOWLEDGMENTS

Portions of this book have appeared in *Aufgabe*, *H_NGM_N*, *N/A Journal*, and *The Volta*. Thank you to the editors of these publications.

For various forms of essential support, thank you to Cassandra Weston, Gary Heidt, Elisa Gabbert, Susan Howe, Joseph Massey, Caroline Larabell, Randall Potts, Katie Peterson, Todd Shalom and Renny Pritikin.

Thank you to Matvei Yankelevich, Daniel Owen and everyone at UDP for their attention and commitment to my work; to Rusty Kinnicutt for the encouragement and patience; and to Darcie Dennigan and Kate Schapira for their significant contributions to this book and dedication to our continuous collective efforts.

"I Mean" is for Sarah Anne Cox.

"The Needle" is for Renny Pritikin.